Tortoises

By Chuck Miller

STECK-VAUGHN
ELEMENTARY · SECONDARY · ADULT · LIBRARY

A Harcourt Company

www.steck-vaughn.com

ANIMALS OF THE RAIN FOREST

Printed and bound in the United States of America
1 2 3 4 5 6 7 8 9 10 WZ 05 04 03 02

Photo Acknowledgments
Heidi Snell, cover; Root Resources/Kenneth Fink, title page; A.B. Sheldon, 12, 22; Ben
Goldstein; The Roving Tortoise/Tui De Roy, 6, 11, 18, 21, 24, 26, 27–28; Visuals
Unlimited/Richard Carlton, 8; Ken Lucas, 16.

Editor: Bryon Cahill
Consultant: Sean Dolan

Content Consultant:
Heather Snell, Charles Darwin Research Station, Galapagos Islands

This book supports the National Science Standards.

Contents

CENTRAL
AMERICA

Gulf of Mexico

VENEZUELA

Pacific Ocean

COLOMBIA

GALAPAGOS
ISLANDS

ECUADOR

PERU

BRAZIL

BOLIVIA

Range of the
Galapagos
Giant Tortoise

Surrounding
Land

Water

Borders

N
W — E
S

CHILE

4

A Quick Look at Tortoises

What do tortoises look like?

Tortoises have tough skin that covers their legs and head. The rest of their body is inside a hard shell. Most tortoises are colored dull brown, gray, green, or yellow. Some tortoises have bright-colored shells and skin.

Where do tortoises live?

Tortoises live all over the world, except very cold places like Antarctica. Many tortoises live in Africa and Madagascar. The largest tortoises in the world live on the Galapagos Islands off the coast of Ecuador.

What do tortoises eat?

Most tortoises eat mainly plants. They eat leaves, plants, grass, and fruit. Other tortoises eat insects, snails, and meat from dead animals that they find.

This Galapagos tortoise has its head pulled inside its shell.

Tortoises in the Rain Forest

Tortoises are among the oldest reptiles on Earth. A reptile is a **cold-blooded** animal with a backbone. Cold-blooded animals have a body temperature that changes, depending on what the temperature is outside.

The tortoise is different from most reptiles because it has a shell. This hard outer covering protects its body. The shell is made up of three parts, the top and bottom shell and the bridge. The bridge connects the top and bottom shell. Most of the tortoise's body fits inside the shell. The shell has two openings, one for the tortoise's head and one for its four legs and tail.

Tortoises belong to a group whose scientific name is Testudines. This name comes from testa, a Latin word that means shell.

Tortoises like these gopher tortoises need to live in warm places.

Where Do Tortoises Live?

Tortoises live in most warm areas of the world. They would freeze in cold areas because they are cold-blooded. Many tortoises live in rain forests and fields in Africa and Madagascar. A rain forest is a warm place where many different types of trees and plants grow close together, and a lot of rain falls.

Some tortoises live on islands. Galapagos tortoises live in the wet highland forests and the drier areas of the Galapagos Islands. Because there is so much food to eat, the Galapagos tortoises that live in the highland areas grow much larger than those that do not.

The trees and plants in the rain forests help tortoises hide from **predators**. Predators are animals that hunt other animals and eat them. Snakes, rats, wild dogs, pigs, cats, birds, and other animals will catch and eat tortoises.

Tortoises have an important role in the rain forest. They eat rain forest fruits and plants. Some of the seeds from these fruits and plants leave their bodies as waste. Waste is what the body does not use or need from food that has been eaten. As tortoises move through rain forests, they spread the seeds to new places. New plants grow from the seeds.

Tortoises also help other animals in the rain forest. Some tortoises will let birds land on their legs and neck. The birds eat insects that are on the tortoise's skin. Many of these insects are harmful to tortoises. Still, the insects are an important food for the birds.

How Are Tortoises Different from Other Turtles?

Tortoises are turtles that live almost all of their life on land. They go to water only to drink it, if they are thirsty. Other turtles live most of their life in water.

The shape of the shell is different, too. Other turtles have a flat shell that helps them swim easier. Because they do not swim, many tortoises have a high shell shaped like half of a ball. Tortoises often live longer than other turtles do.

The feet and legs of a tortoise are not like the legs of a turtle. Turtles have long, thin legs. They have webbed feet on the end of their legs like ducks do. This helps them swim easily. Tortoises have thick, short legs that help them move more easily on land. They do not have webbed feet. Instead, hard, tough skin covers their feet. The tough skin lets them walk over rough places without their feet getting hurt. Their toenails help them grip as they climb over rocks and logs.

You can see the high, rounded shell of this tortoise.

▲ This red-footed tortoise is one of the most colorful species of tortoise.

What Do Tortoises Look Like?

There are more than 40 **species** of tortoise, and many of them look very much alike. A species is a group of animals or plants that share common features and are closely related to each other.

Each tortoise species has its own style of shell. Shells can be unusual shapes with bumps and curves. Some are very hard and feel like a rock. Others are much softer and feel like leather.

Shells can be different colors, too. Most tortoises in the rain forest have green, brown, or yellow shells. These colors help camouflage the tortoises. **Camouflage** is special coloring or patterns that help an animal blend in with its surroundings. The camouflage helps tortoises hide among the plants and trees of the rain forest.

The red-footed tortoise lives in the rain forests of South America. Unlike many tortoises, the red-footed tortoise is very brightly colored. It has spots of bright red and yellow on the skin that cover its head and legs.

Tortoises use their shell to stay safe from predators. If a tortoise senses danger, it pulls its legs and head inside its shell. It sometimes uses its legs to cover its face when in danger, too.

The size of the tortoise depends on the species. The speckled tortoise is the smallest. It rarely grows larger than 3.5 inches (8.9 cm). Galapagos tortoises are the largest tortoises. They can weigh more than 600 pounds (300 kg).

This Galapagos tortoise is drinking water from a puddle.

What Tortoises Eat

Many tortoises are herbivores. Herbivores eat only plants. The tortoises who live in the rain forest eat the leaves and fruit of plants and trees that grow there.

Some tortoises that live in the rain forest are **omnivores**. Omnivores are animals that eat both plants and animals. These rain forest tortoises eat snails, insects, and worms. They may also eat the meat from dead animals they find.

Tortoises can find water to drink in many ways. They drink water from a puddle on the rain forest ground or from a stream or lake. They also drink water from the leaves of a plant that grow close to the ground. Their body also uses the water from the moist food that they eat.

⚡ **This grazing tortoise is eating grass.**

Finding and Eating Food

Some tortoise species, such as the red-footed and the leopard, are grazers. Grazers are always eating whatever they can find, usually grass and leaves that are on the ground. Other tortoise species, such as the Galapagos, are browsers. Browsers pick and choose what they eat. They usually have longer necks. They stretch their necks so they can reach leaves and fruits that grow on bushes and short trees.

Tortoises do not have teeth. They have sharp edges around their mouths called a beak. Meat-eating tortoises catch and cut up prey with their beak. Prey is an animal hunted as food. Herbivorous tortoises use their beak to cut up plants.

Tortoises swallow their food whole. They use saliva to wet the food to make it easier to swallow. Saliva is a watery mixture made in the mouth. Tortoises use enzymes to **digest** the food in their stomach. To digest means to break down food so the body can use it. Enzymes are liquids in their stomach that break apart pieces of food.

Like all reptiles, it takes a long time for tortoises to turn their food into energy that their bodies can use. This means they do not have to eat as often as other animals do. Most tortoises eat several times a week. If no food is around, they can go without eating for even longer periods of time.

Galapagos tortoises like to eat, but they do not need to eat much. They can also store a lot of water in their body. Scientists believe these tortoises can live up to one year without eating or drinking water.

These two males are about to fight with each other.

A Tortoise's Life Cycle

Female and male tortoises usually do not live together. They gather together during mating season. Some tortoises mate once a year. Others mate more often.

Tortoises mate only with other tortoises from their own species. They can tell other members of their species by the color and shape of the shell. When a male finds a female, he bobs his head up and down or side to side. He makes special noises. Each species makes its own kind of noise. Some sound like chickens clucking. Other noises sound like grunts or low growls.

During mating season, male tortoises may fight one another for females. Some male tortoises fight by crashing their shells into one another. The winner knocks the other male over and then gets to mate with the female.

Young Tortoises

After mating, female tortoises look for good places to lay their eggs. They find a sunny place with loose, moist soil. If the location does not receive sunlight, the eggs will not hatch. Once they have found a place, females dig holes in the ground. They lay their eggs in the holes. The number of eggs a female lays depends on the species. Some females lay more than 100 eggs. Some lay just one. A group of tortoise eggs is called a clutch.

After laying eggs in the holes, females bury the eggs loosely with soil. This helps keep the eggs warm. It also hides the eggs from predators. Birds and snakes may try to find and eat the eggs.

Most females leave the eggs soon after they lay them. Some females guard the eggs. They fight predators that might try to eat the eggs.

Young tortoises grow inside the eggs. They hatch several months after their mother has laid her eggs. The young tortoises break out of the eggshells using a horny tip on the end of their nose. Then, they dig their way above ground.

This tortoise is hatching from its egg.

Their mother is gone, and they must know what to do to survive. There are many dangers waiting for them. Predators eat many newly hatched tortoises before they have a chance to grow up.

Most tortoises live to be more than 10 or 15 years old. Galapagos tortoises can live to be more than 100 years old.

▲ **This leopard tortoise is basking in the sun.**

A Tortoise's Day

Most tortoises begin their day when the sun comes up. They crawl into the sunlight to warm themselves. Then, they lie in the sun. This is called **basking**. Basking helps them to raise their body temperature because they are cold-blooded. Warmer body temperatures help them digest their food. When there is no food, tortoises stay cool and inactive because this uses up less energy.

This is how they can live so long without eating or drinking.

When they are warm, tortoises become more active. They then begin looking for food by walking across the rain forest floor.

By noon, it usually becomes hotter. Since they are cold-blooded, tortoises get hotter, too. Tortoises will die if they become too hot. So, they move out of the sun and into the shade of plants and trees. Many tortoises sit in water or roll in the wet mud to cool off. They also seem to enjoy being in the rain.

Tortoises need to stay warm at night, or they will lose the body heat they got from the sun. Some dig holes called **burrows**. They crawl inside their burrows to stay warm. Other tortoises move into a mud puddle to sleep for the night. The mud coats their body and helps them hold in heat.

If it becomes too hot or dry, tortoises can **estivate**. Estivate means to spend the summer in a sleeplike state. When a tortoise is estivating, it usually crawls into its burrow and stays still. This helps it save its energy so it does not need to eat or drink. It can estivate for months at a time. The tortoise becomes active again when it rains or the weather cools.

These tortoises are keeping cool by lying in this mud puddle.

The Future of Tortoises

There were once hundreds of species of tortoise. Now, many species have become extinct. Extinct means there are no animals of that kind left alive in the wild.

Many giant tortoises became extinct because they were hunted and eaten as food. Sailors used to catch giant tortoises. They turned the tortoises upside down and stacked them on top of each other in their ships. The tortoises could live up to a year like that, without eating or drinking. The sailors ate the tortoises for fresh meat when they got hungry during their trips.

Today, many tortoises are in danger of becoming extinct. People still hunt tortoises. They eat tortoise meat and make belts and boots out of tortoise skin. Other people use the shells to make combs and eyeglass frames.

These children are learning about Galapagos tortoises.

What Will Happen to Tortoises?

To protect tortoises, new laws are being created in many countries where tortoises live. It is against the law to hunt or sell tortoises as pets in these countries.

Some scientists take male and female tortoises out of the wild. They bring them to zoos to

Tortoises do not sweat like human beings do. The skin on their legs is covered with scales. These small, rough pieces of skin help tortoises keep water in their body.

breed them. Breeding means to keep animals and plants, to produce more of them. Scientists do this so there will be more tortoises in the future. Young tortoises are protected so they can grow up to mate.

Most tortoises born in captivity cannot live in the rain forest. They will die because they do not know how to find food there. Scientists try to teach these tortoises how to find food and hide better in the rain forest. Then, they release the tortoises back into the wild. This is called repatriation.

People who try to save tortoises hope that breeding and repatriation will lead to more wild tortoises in the future. Many people understand that tortoises are important to life in the rain forest. They must teach other people what they know. Then tortoises can live in the rain forests for a long time.

shell
see page 7

head
see page 7

legs
see page 10

Glossary

basking (BAS-king)—getting warm by lying under heat, like the sun

burrows (BUR-ohs)—holes or tunnels in the ground where an animal lives

camouflage (KAM-o-flaj)—colors, shapes, and patterns that make something blend in with its background

cold-blooded (KOHLD BLUHD-id)—animals with body temperatures that change according to their surroundings

digest (dye-JEST)—to break down food so the body can use it

estivate (ESS-ti-vayt)—to rest in a sleeplike state

omnivores (AHM-nee-vohrs)—animals that eat both plants and animals

predators (PRED-uh-turs)—animals that hunt other animals for food

species (SPEE-sees)—a group of animals or plants most closely related to each other in the scientific classification system

Internet Sites

Galapagos Tortoises
students.washcoll.edu/Student.Pages/
  Karen.Sieger/galapago.htm

Restoring the Tortoise Dynasty
www.darwinfoundation.org/Restoring/
  index.html

Useful Address

California Turtle and Tortoise Club
P.O. Box 7300
Van Nuys, CA 91409-7300

Books to Read

Gerholdt, James E. *Turtles and Tortoises.* Edina, MN: Abdo & Daughters, 1994.

Hawxhurst, Joan C. *Turtles and Tortoises.* San Diego, CA: Lucent Books, 2001.

Index